TWICE THE MAN

A photographic diary of a year in the life of the Grenadier Guards

This book is dedicated to the memory of the Grenadiers
killed in Afghanistan in late 2009 and early 2010:

WO1 (RSM) Darren Chant
Sgt Matthew Telford
L/Sgt Dave Greenhalgh
Guardsman Jimmy Major
Guardsman Jamie Janes

Gone but not forgotten.

WO1 (RSM) Darren Chant and Queens Coy Sgt Mjr
Williams chat in the staging area before the exercise starts.

CONTENTS

FOREWORD

BRIGADIER DAVID MADDAN, THE REGIMENTAL LIEUTENANT COLONEL

This book is a vivid portrait of the Grenadier Guards taken over the course of 2009 and 2010. The centrepiece is the deployment of the First Battalion to Afghanistan. The photographs capture the personal experience of Grenadiers serving their country in the most difficult of circumstances. They provide a glimpse of the exceptionally strong camaraderie as well as the tension, exhaustion, strain, humour and humanity that is the enduring experience of soldiers on operations.

The operational deployment is set within the context of the broader sweep of Regimental life, showing how Grenadiers are able to combine excellence on operations with the twin commitment of ceremonial duties. The Presentation of Colours and The Queen's Birthday Parade both took place less than three months after the return from Helmand and while the memories of the tour were very fresh. The pictures of the wounded attending parades are particularly poignant and remind us all of the human cost of service.

The 65th anniversary commemoration of the capture of the bridge at Nijmegen in September 1944, in which Nijmegen Company and the Regimental Band played a leading role, and Regimental Remembrance Day are reminders of the importance of our history and how the service of Grenadiers in the past is honoured by the current generation.

I am confident that you will find that Algy Brinton has captured the essence of the Regiment over a typically varied period. The enduring characteristic of Grenadiers achieving the highest standards in all that they do comes across most clearly of all.

Brigadier David Maddan and Major Grant Baker look on as Nijmegen Company march into position for the parade.

1 PRE-DEPLOYMENT TRAINING
OTTERBURN, UK

We were the last 11 Light Brigade unit (of ten Major Units) to enter into the Pre-Deployment Training (PDT) programme. We had barely dusted ourselves off from Exercise GRAND PRIX 6 (a demanding overseas exercise in the Kenyan bush) and deployed straight into it. A slightly formulaic process, one size inevitably does not fit all due to resource constraints (training areas, equipment etc), so it is managed as a best effort by the Brigade Headquarters against concurrent changes in theatre.

Fourteen weeks sounds innocuous enough and looks deceptively so on an Excel spreadsheet. Just how much can be programmed into 98 training days (including weekends)? The answer is an awful lot – so much so that the majority of Guardsmen look forward to the tour because they know it means PDT must end! Our own particular journey began at 1200hrs on a cold Monday in April 2009 in Longmoor Training Camp, Hampshire, with the Tactical Commanders' Cadre (TCC). A five-day briefing and tactical training period for all Junior Non-Commissioned Officers (JNCOs) and

above, it is the foundation for all subsequent training, where the skills are taught to be passed on to all ranks, the so-called 'Cascade Training'. The journey ended in early August 2009 in the vast expanse of Otterburn Training Area in Northumberland, where each Rifle Company Group executed a Combined Arms Live Firing Exercise (CALFEX) on a scale not seen in training before the UK's involvement in Afghanistan.

The Battalion's PDT period – an intense experience for all who undertake it – is memorable for many reasons. The ones that stick are: the busman's holiday of all the major UK training areas; the 'beasting' Battalion Headquarters took to make it all happen; the two weeks of State Ceremonial undertaken in the middle (remember – 'Twice The Man' in the Grenadiers!); the sobering events of the commanders' recce to Afghanistan; the ingenuity of Battalion staff officers during Brigade training events ('feeding the beast'!); and the excellent visit of HRH The Colonel to Thetford and the Afghan village.

Engaging targets at between 100 to 150 metres.
This Queen's Company gun team's tracer rounds are ignited as they pass through the targets and ricochet into the night sky.

Schermulys silhouette
Company Sergeant Major Steve Williams, his quad and a Jackal.

Members of The Queen's Company watch over the supposed Forward Line of Enemy Troops.

Members of The Queen's Company pepperpot across open ground as Targets pop up.

Targets up.

An Apache Longbow provides air support as troops from The Queen's Company move up in dead ground.

Members of Support Company clear and hold a sheep pen to provide fire support for 2 Company to advance.

Guardsmen of No 2 Platoon, The Queen's Company, rest for a moment in a house they've just cleared.

NIJMEGEN COMPANY: 65TH ANNIVERSARY OF THE BATTLE OF NIJMEGEN

NIJMEGEN, HOLLAND

On a glorious late summer's day on 20 September 2009, the Dutch town of Nijmegen (the oldest city in the Netherlands) commemorated the 65th anniversary of the Battle of Nijmegen. Since the Arnhem Commemorations were meant to be the 'main effort', planning for a low key event had started earlier in the year with the Mayor of Nijmegen inviting Nijmegen Company, Grenadier Guards to attend; as it happened, the Regimental Band was scheduled to play at an event in Belgium the night before the Commemoration, so the offer was gratefully accepted that the Band should play at the Commemoration. Finally, it emerged that Prince Philip, our Colonel, was willing to attend, at which point Her Majesty Queen Beatrix of the Netherlands decided that she would be there to greet him. Thus 'low key' turned 'high profile'!

Lord Carrington drove out to Holland on the Saturday, attended by his 'ADC' (and godson) Major Lord Valentine Cecil and The Colonel 'popped over' from Balmoral for the afternoon on Sunday. In mid-afternoon Nijmegen Company, carrying The Queen's Company Colour, along with the Regimental Band, provided a Guard of Honour for HM Queen Beatrix and HRH The Colonel. Once the Royal Party had inspected the Guard of Honour, they took their seats for the Commemoration; the Mayor of Nijmegen presented medals to Lord Carrington and the Lieutenant Colonel, who accepted them on behalf of the Guards Armoured Division and the Regiment, and to representatives of the US 82nd Airborne Division. Peter Carrington spoke with great eloquence and then wreaths were laid, followed by speeches. After the Commemoration, HM Queen Beatrix and The Colonel walked down the ranks of Nijmegen Company chatting to the Guardsmen as they went. At the same time, veterans were boarding a convoy of military vehicles, headed by a Sherman tank, ready to process across the Bridge.

HM Queen Beatrix and HRH The Colonel watched the Procession, led by the Regimental Band and Nijmegen Company as they set off to march across the bridge. Thereafter, the Royal Party departed, whilst the remainder of the spectators watched as the procession returned and headed towards the Town Hall for a most enjoyable reception which was given by the City of Nijmegen.

It was a very happy day, with hundreds of veterans and thousands of Dutch spectators turning out for the event. Of course, the jollity of the occasion did not obscure the fact that we were commemorating a bloody battle fought against a ruthless and determined enemy. In his brief speech, Peter Carrington recalled the battle, the 'fog of war' the courage of those who took part, and particularly the courage of the Dutch people both during the battle and the harsh winter that followed.

It is humbling to see how, to this day, the inhabitants of those western European countries which were liberated by the British and American forces remain enormously grateful for the sacrifice that was made for them; the Dutch are notable in this respect, and particularly the interest of the young in the events of 65 years ago. The Commemoration of the 65th anniversary of the Battle of Nijmegen was a poignant event but, as should be the case, was a thoroughly enjoyable occasion.

A Guardsman puts the finishing touches to his curb chain on the eve of the parade.

The Lieutenant Colonel Brigadier David Maddan and Major Grant Baker receiving HM Queen Beatrix and HRH The Colonel.

Nijmegen Company presenting arms and lowering the Royal Standard of the Regiment in the presence of HM Queen Beatrix and HRH The Colonel.

Major Edward Paintin leads Nijmegen Company over the bridge that gave them their name.

After parading through the town, Nijmegen Company halts at the foot of the steps to the Town Hall.

Brigadier David Maddan talks with General Petraeus as the General's security detail goes about its business.

Weapons are counted and recounted after the parade.

NIJMEGEN COMPANY: INSTALLATION OF THE NEW CONSTABLE
TOWER OF LONDON, LONDON

'The installation of the new Constable of the Tower of London was possibly one of the most spectacular ceremonies I have participated in whilst doing State Ceremonial Duties. The backdrop of the White Tower set against the night sky, the assembled masses on the rain-soaked stands and the ceremonial regalia of those on parade on the immaculately kept green, provide a very fitting setting for this auspicious event.

'To be involved in the installation of General Sir Richard Dannatt as the 159th Constable of Her Majesty's oldest and most renowned palace and fortress was a great honour, not least because it is an event which occurs so infrequently.

'We managed to get the last-minute rehearsals completed, with all the required participants, a few hours before and as ever the assembled military personnel took it all in their stride and produced an exemplary performance, not least the very young Guardsmen within the Company, some of whom had only just finished their initial training.

'The ceremony involved the handing over of the gold master keys of the Tower by the Lord Chamberlain, on behalf of Her Majesty The Queen, symbolizing the Constable's responsibility for this Royal Palace. Nijmegen Company had the privilege of providing the Guard of Honour alongside the Yeoman Warders, The Honourable Artillery Company and The Royal Fusiliers and I, as the Company Commander of the Guard of Honour, had the privilege of commanding the parade.

'This occasion will possibly stand out in history as one of the wettest ceremonies ever, with the almost torrential rain only adding to the atmosphere and drama of this event.'

Nijmegen Company, 'caped up', marches on the slippery cobbles in front of Tower Bridge.

C/Sgt Philip Childs looks over the parading troops.

The heavy rain brings the night in quickly as Nijmegen Company forms up.

Raindrops are flung from Nijmegen Company's weapons as they present arms.

General Sir Richard Dannatt (now Lord Dannatt) is installed as the 159th Constable of the Tower.

4 GRENADIER GUARDS BATTLEGROUP
HELMAND PROVINCE, AFGHANISTAN

'We are in Afghanistan with the rest of 11 Light Brigade, spread between Nad-e Ali District and Lashkar-Gah. With over 100,000 people in 250km^2 of intricately farmed Green Zone as a backdrop, there is a pretty active insurgency in Nad-e Ali. Lashkar-Gah is a sprawling city which seems more peaceful but could easily flare up. This area is the starting point for a large Afghan and International Security Assistance Force effort to clear the insurgents from Central Helmand, so we knew we will be at the heart of things.

'Conditions are rough and rudimentary. Most of us live in a network of patrol bases which are local Afghan compounds improved with some barriers and sentry positions, in the heart of the local community. Food is mainly rations, self-cooked. Water comes from local boreholes or is shipped in on supply convoys. We wash using wash bowls and shower bags, and sleep on camp beds. The routine is busy, noisy, dusty…and dangerous. The majority of the time is spent out and about on patrol reassuring the local population, or on deliberate offensive operations to disrupt the insurgents. The weights we carry come as a shock – routinely over 70 lbs – essential equipment, body armour, weapons, ammunition, batteries, water, and food. Comforts are hard to come by – a few satellite phones at best. Mail is delivered whenever the supply convoys come through, which for some people in the more remote patrol bases is not that often.'

Early morning training, doing laps at Brigade Headquaters FOB SHAWQUAT.

Gdsm Babacarr Silva and Gdsm Richard Addai relax after a vehicle patrol.

Sgt Dean Bailey talks to members of 5 Platoon.

Gdsm Michael Shearer and Gdsm Christopher Mellor / No 2 Company, Blue 22

'Glad I am not going through this alone and have my mates here with me – but I can't wait to be back home with my friends and family.'

L/Cpl Joseph (Disco) Dicastiglione, Gdsm Chris Taylor, Gdsm John Shields / No 2 Company, Blue 22

'Well, being out here for the second time meant that I had experienced it before and so was ready for what was coming. I enjoy it, it's my job …!'

Whilst the Commanding Officer meets with local police and some US troops, Gdsm Krishna Murray takes a moment.

Troops relieved from a desert OP patrol back through the graveyard using a metal detector to clear their path.

L/Cpl Ben Marchant enjoying a brief break in the sun.

L/Cpl Joseph (Disco) Dicastiglione waits for the arrival of the Prime Minister.

Flanked by the Prime Minister's entourage, Colonel Roly Walker briefs Gordon Brown on the current situation.

Colonel Roly Walker, Brigadier James Cowan and Lieutenant General Simon Mayall CB (DCDS Operations).

Sergeant Major Ian Farrell / Headquarter Company, SHAWQUAT

'To be on Operations is a high point in any soldier's career. Having served in a number of countries around the world, I can say that Afghanistan is without doubt the most challenging. As the Sergeant Major, the senior Non-Commissioned soldier within the Battlegroup, I relish the challenge of leadership that Operations bring – it's a real honour for me.'

Major Rich Green / Company Commander No 2 Company, SHAWQUAT

'An amazing experience with most of the greatest highs and lows of my life. From the tragedy of losing Guardsman Jamie Janes, to the pride of witnessing the amazing courage of the whole Company Group in WAHID and our greatest success of the tour being the transition in Chah-e-Mirza. I was truly honoured to command Number Two Company and I thank them for that.'

The Quartermaster's Department get set to receive a heli resupply.

Colonel Roly Walker and the Senior Major, Major Andrew James, host the nightly conference.

L/Sgt Aidan O'Brien by a wall near five strikes.

L/Cpl Ben Marchant waiting to go out on patrol.

Weekly deep clean of Patrol Weapons.

Each man carries weapons, ammunition, body armour, water and other
essential equipment that weighs in excess of 85lbs.

Sgt Paul Housby rests in the shade of a compound during a patrol in the village of Washir.

Sgt Paul Housby, L/Cpl Ben Marchant, L/Cpl Martin Moore, L/Cpl Ben Middleton, L/Sgt Aidan O'Brien / The Queen's Company, Tapa Parang

'My daily routine consists of waking up about 0600hrs, boiling some water for a shower, having a shave and some breakfast. Moving up to the Ops room for the daily tasking and patrol schedule. Most days I'm looking at 3–4 patrols each lasting from 2–6 hrs dependent on the distance and task as well as any complications which come out of the patrol – ie finding an IED or gathering some hot Intel which needs to be followed up quickly. The days are long and knackering but it's good to know that we control our area of operations because of our robust patrolling and interaction with the locals. We continue to deny the enemy freedom of movement.'

Gdsm Robert Bligdon and Gdsm Shane Galvin / The Queen's Company, Tapa Parang

'From clearing IEDs and being caught in firefights to gathering information and providing security for the locals, the job out here is
definitely challenging and varied, but there is so much reward in seeing how much of a difference we have made and continue to make.'

Soft hats on patrol.
A lone Gdsm takes up position on the corner of a compound.

Radio Check.
Sgt Galvin (USMC), Sgt Paul Housby and Sgt Rodriguez (USMC).

Afghan National Army personnel pause for a while, whilst an ITN film crew interviews locals who are rebuilding the Nad Ali schoolhouse.

Gdsm Madou Jallow eyeballs a jovial local crowd.

The Joint Grenadier/USMC patrol heads past the local motorbike garage,
along the canal back towards Tapa P.

An unknown guardsman chats with a local boy whilst on patrol near Blue 22.

A few moments of calm before heading out on night patrol.

Ready to go.

L/Sgt Dwain Oliver gives Orders before leading his patrol out into the night.

Lieutenant James Taylor spends his evening writing up that day's patrol report.

Just another night in Helmand.

Gdsm Daniel Rollason / The Queen's Company, Tapa Parang, Check Point North

'Being my second time in Afghanistan, it has been slightly easier than my first
because of past experiences, but more has happened.'

Gdsm David Worman and Gdsm Aron Carey / The Queen's Company, Tapa Parang, Check Point North

'Afghanistan could be hard at times but it was always made so much easier by the lads I was with.
I had good friends out there and we were all brought closer by our experiences.'

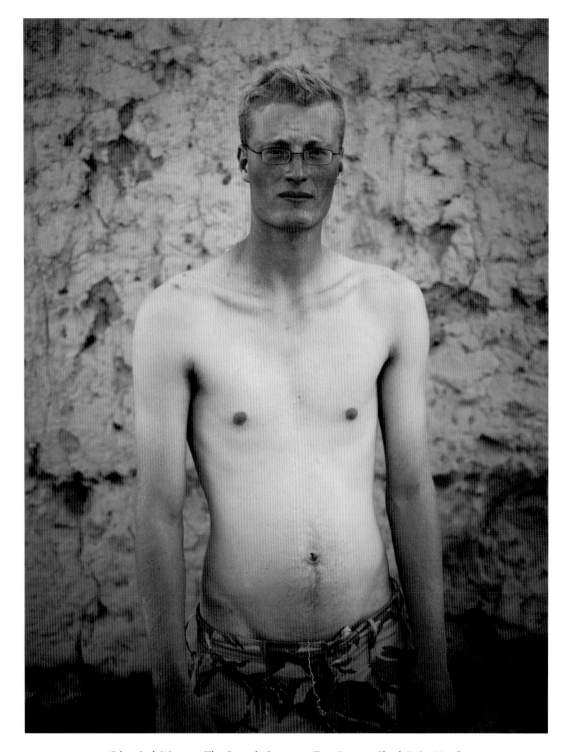

Gdsm Jack Warner / The Queen's Company, Tapa Parang, Check Point North

'It's been a long hot day.'

Gdsm Dou Dou Gomez / The Queen's Company, Tapa Parang, Check Point North

'Out here it is incredibly challenging at the end of the day, but we have achieved our mission on behalf of the Company,
and it has been a very good experience working with our lads on the front line.'

Captain Neil England / Headquarter Company, Tapa Parang

'Logistically, sustaining a Battlegroup of this size is very much a team effort. It is a never-ending challenge
which tests one's ability to remain flexible, whilst always focused on the main effort.'

Major Alex Cartwright / The Captain of The Queen's Company, Tapa Parang

'The Company is involved in the full spectrum of counter-insurgency operations, from confrontations with the Taliban to construction projects and shuras with locals. Working alongside the Afghan National Police and Afghan National Army is quite an experience – it greatly increases our local understanding and the characters mean there is never a dull moment.'

Some of the boys from No 1 Platoon, The Queen's Company, Check Point South.

Afghan National Policemen relax on the roof of the compound in the early evening light at Check Point South.

Gdsm Kyle Walkden, Gdsm Carl McClendon and Gdsm Christian Heaton (Sitting) / The Inkerman Company, Washir Check Point

'Being out here in Afghanistan has been the weirdest experience of my life: exciting, stressful, scary, sometimes you're bored out of your mind ... but you have a right laugh with your mates!'

One of the innumerable pets adopted by the boys.

Gdsm Jonathan Plant / The Inkerman Company, Washir Check Point

'Time in the FOB is slow and frustrating at times. One of the toughest things
for me on this tour was being away from my wife and family. I missed them very much.'

Gdsm Paul Hemsley / The Inkerman Company, Washir Check Point

'Two days after that MASTIFF was blown up we then went to do the same move: the recce call sign was going out to recce us a new route to take, but we had to get the equipment to the FOB none the less. We got just past where we were IED'd last time and we thought we were home and dry, but just as a commander was saying "if we make it over" we got blown up again. The GPMG and my MASTIFF were both u/s – there was no bar armour on the front of the Mastiff and my ear was still ringing for hours after – but luckily no one was injured or hurt at all. We then radioed back to FOB Price to call the LED out again and got them to pick up our MASTIFF. We then got into another MASTIFF and went back to FOB Price.'

Soaking up some rays.

A young guardsman relaxes in the early evening sun.

Gdsm Matt Cox

'I am part of a 32-man recce platoon. So far we have had a good tour. We have been moved about a lot over the Nad-e Ali district – some of our missions include going past the forward line of enemy troops and getting a detailed knowledge of their situation and what transport they use to get around, as well as their main routes in and out of our area of interest. We have all worked extremely hard on this tour and I think I can speak for every bloke and say we are looking forward to returning back to England and seeing our family – and hopefully not taking part in Trooping the Colour.'

Padre Jason Clarke / Zarghun Kalay

'The role of the Padre is to love your men and women. Today my mind is filled with thoughts of those no longer with us.
I watch the lads lifting weights and cooking their scoff and as I watch I pray for each one of them. They do not know and I will not
tell them, but every day I pray for them.'

Gdsm Scott Beekman, L/Cpl Ross Wescott and Sgt Brian Patterson / The Queen's Company, Check Point South

'Afghanistan is a physically and mentally challenging place to work which I have enjoyed very much.
It's been good working so closely with all my friends. Although I'm sure the flight out of here will be the best bit!
That and putting rocks in the Platoon Commander's daysack before a patrol.'

The Commanding Officer's party takes a break during a large shura at Sharzad.

Sharzad.

4am. Out on Patrol.

While we wait for the road clearance operation to begin,
troops from The Inkerman Company negotiate with a local man for temporary use of his compound.

This Gunner takes a moment to pause as the advance slows.

Patrolling in the early morning sunshine.

L/Cpl Alexander Rigby listening intently to the comms.

Two weeks earlier this wheat would have been ankle high.
Two weeks later it will be nearing shoulder height.

L/Sgt Daniel Marsden, Gdsm Keith Rolatt / The Inkerman Company, Sharzad

'I have returned to my company after a short stint with the Estonian Infantry in Pimon and Wahid as a MASTIFF commander. The Inkerman Company is based in Shazad (Nad-e Ali) and the experience is very different from that of OP HERRICK 6, due to the time of year and also changes in enemy tactics. Having to tackle IEDs is a regular occurrence, along with exchanges of fire with the enemy, which makes any progress a long-drawn-out process. With the great efforts of The Inkerman Company and the Battlegroup as a whole, we are achieving our mission in clearing and securing our district by pushing the enemy out and helping the locals within.'

Gdsm Robert Hollis, Gdsm Ryan Rowbottom / The Inkerman Company, Sharzad

'The best and worst time of mine and all the blokes' careers – and Lucy's life.
She is the puppy we adopted and looked after through our tour.'

Lieutenant James Brown of the Queen's Company taking the opportunity for personal administration.

The guys of No 5 Platoon, No 2 Company, training hard to stay in shape and relieve their boredom.

'The Captain', as The Queen's Company Commander is known, back briefs the Company Sergeant Major.

Members of The Queen's Company take a well-earned break to throw some arrows.

Lieutenant Mike Dobbin of The Queen's Company greets the local chief of police.

A policeman sits guard at the police station entrance as members of The Queen's Company
audit the number of weapons recently given to the ANP.

Afghan National Army, Afghan National Police, Grenadiers, and civilians rest in the shade of a
compound wall whilst the compound is searched for arms and drugs by the ANP.

Business as usual in Nad-e Ali district centre.

ANA Commander takes a chai break in Tapa Parang.

An Afghan family is briefly held up as an IED is removed and destroyed.

Members of No 5 Platoon of No 2 Company push out from their CP to conduct a joint ISAF-ANP
patrol along the canal that splits the Western edge of Nad-e Ali and the desert.

Members of The Queen's Company put in an impromptu checkpoint.

Gdsm Christopher Taylor patrolling out to spend a few days in the desert OP that gives this 2 platoon callsign overwatch of the dead ground stretching away from their checkpoint.

Silhouetted in the early morning light, this young Grenadier stands on a ladder to get a better view over a compound wall.

A memorial for a fallen comrade: L/Sgt Dave Greenhalgh, The Queen's Company, KIA.

5 MEDALS PARADE
WELLINGTON BARRACKS, LONDON

'We have only been back for a few days and it's time for the
Medals Parade in Wellington Barracks. This is a very significant day
for us. Our families and friends have turned out to mark our return
from operations. All the Companies will parade, and Campaign
Medals will be presented to those who were on their first tour to
Afghanistan, and The Major General will present medals to a few of
our wounded who are able to join us.

'This will be followed by a Service in the Guards Chapel
which will give us time to reflect on and remember those from the
Battlegroup who were killed or wounded in Afghanistan, and for
individuals to remember the highs and lows of the tour.

'We will finish the day with a reception for the Battalion and
families.

This day brings Operation HERRICK 11 to a close.'

The Medals.

The young men of the Battalion are presented with their medals.

The Battalion lines up for the parade.

The Battalion reforms into its normal ORBAT.

The Sgt Major and the Adjutant with some of the men who received injuries on their recent tour of Afghanistan.

The Families.

A memorial to the Fallen amidst the bustle of the present.

Gdsm Alasan Ceesay and his family.

Gdsm Steven Holley, his mother and L/Cpl Jonathan Pearce.

The troops celebrate with their loved ones.

The young officers retire to the Mess.

6 1ST BATTALION GRENADIER GUARDS: PRESENTATION OF NEW COLOURS

LONDON

The Colours are the encompassing symbol of a Battalion. They represent the history, tradition, sacrifice and bravery off all those who served and are still serving in the Battalion. There are two Colours presented, the Queen's Colour and the Regimental Colour, the Queen's Colour being only carried when Her Majesty or another member of the Royal Family is present. They are treated at all times with the utmost respect and follow the Battalion wherever in the world it may be deployed. It is a very special occasion when a Battalion receives New Colours, occurring only every ten years or so.

As the Old Colours were marched off parade, there was time for those present to reflect on all that had happened over the previous months and think of those who had not returned with the Battalion. Shortly afterwards the New Colours were presented by Her Majesty The Queen, having been blessed by the Clergy – a poignant moment for all present as they considered where these Colours might serve with the Battalion in the future.

Only a few weeks before, The First Battalion had been in dusty desert combat kit and body armour in the middle of Helmand province, Afghanistan. However, when the moment arrived, and thanks to hours of hard work by the non-commissioned officers, the Battalion stood proudly in the gardens of Buckingham Palace in immaculate tunics, with the New Colours in pride of place. After overcoming the trickiest of drill movements, removing headdress, the whole Battalion as one gave a stirring three cheers for Her Majesty. For the 1st Battalion, receiving New Colours so soon after returning from operations in Afghanistan along with the knowledge that they would be trooping their Colour on The Queen's Birthday Parade made the day even more memorable.

'Kneeling in front of Her Majesty as she blessed the Colour with a touch of her hand and knowing that in only a few weeks I would be carrying the same Colour as the Ensign on the Birthday Parade was a tremendous moment and a great honour.'

Fresh back from Afghanistan and having had only two weeks' leave,
L/Sgt Roderick Tracey makes the transition look effortless.

The Officers.

The Colours.

Major (Vince) Gaunt helps the inspection party, with his fine attention to detail.

Officers receive their briefing from the Commanding Officer as to how the rehearsal has gone.

Rehearsal.

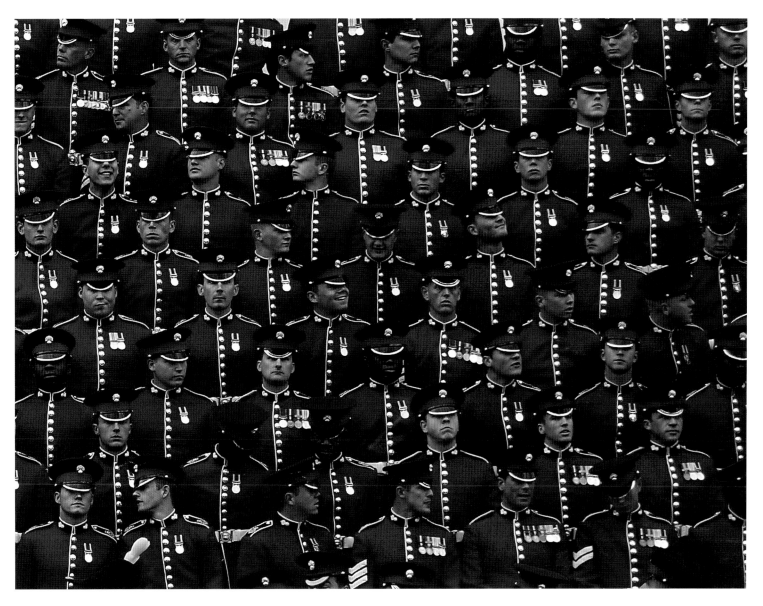

Photograph.

The men stand motionless as HM The Queen approaches to inspect them.

In a drill move you will probably not have seen before, the men remove their bearskins and thrust them aloft during the three cheers for The Queen.

HM The Queen is introduced to RQMS Andrew (Niffy) Hill.

HRH The Colonel chats with the men about their tour.

The New Colours.

HM The Queen and the Battalion sit for the photograph.

7 REGIMENTAL REMEMBRANCE DAY: BLACK SUNDAY

LONDON

Regimental Remembrance Sunday, or 'Black Sunday' as it is sometimes colloquially described, is the day in the year when the family of the Regiment comes together in the Guards Chapel and on Horse Guards Parade to honour those Grenadiers who, since the Regiment was formed, made the supreme sacrifice for monarch and country.

Hundreds of Grenadiers, members of the Association, the First Guards Club and serving Grenadiers of the First Battalion and Nijmegen Company gather in the Guards Chapel for the Remembrance Service. To the plaintive and most moving notes of 'Grenadier's Return' played on fife and drum, wreaths are laid. After the service the parade then forms up on Wellington Barracks square and marches to Horse Guards behind 'the best band in the land', where a wreath is laid on the Guards Memorial. The Regimental Lieutenant Colonel then takes the salute as the parade returns to Wellington Barracks.

After the ceremony, the Association company give three rousing cheers to serving Grenadiers, and the family of the Regiment then moves to respective messes to relax. 'Black Sunday' encapsulates the very ethos of the phrase 'Once a Grenadier always a Grenadier'.

As tradition dictates, the officers parade early at The Grenadier.
Pints, Bloody Marys and perhaps a sausage for breakfast.

Capt Andrew Tiernan and Capt James Harrison / The Grenadier pub, Belgravia

'James and I joined the Army on the same day and were in the same platoon throughout our training at the Royal Military Academy Sandhurst. We commissioned into the Grenadier Guards together. Three years later, on James' last day in the Army in 2008, we were cycling from Canada to Mexico down the west coast of the United States in order to raise money for injured Grenadiers and the bereaved families of lost Grenadiers. And that is what the Regimental Rememberance Day is all about – coming together as a regiment, as a family, in order to remember our fallen comrades. Black Sunday brings the family together. It is very special to march with men who served in the Grenadiers many years ago, and great fun to catch up with friends like James.'

The walk back to Wellington Barracks down a deserted Mall.

Major Grant Baker lays a wreath at the Mareth Cross,
commemorating the Grenadiers of the 5th Battalion who lost their lives at the Battle of Mareth in 1943.

CSM Sebastian Miles chats with CSM Peter Downes.

The old and the new form up shoulder to shoulder.

The wreath is laid.

Heading back to barracks.

Dismissed.

8 CEREMONIAL DUTIES
HORSE GUARDS, LONDON

'There is a saying within the Regiment "Twice the Man in The Grenadiers". Never have truer words been spoken than over the past year. As Op MOSHTERAK reached its final stages on Op HERRICK 11, we were well into the planning for the next phase of the Battlegroup's journey, that of ceremonial duties.

'The return to the UK, we knew, was going to bring fresh challenges, with the presentation of New Colours and The Queen's Birthday Parade. Being the Battalion chosen to Troop its Colour through the ranks of the remainder of the Household Division is always an honour and privilege. Being chosen this year had an even bigger privilege about it and there was an extra excitement about it.

'It was approached as a continuation of the Operation, the next phase. The Battlegroup, still with one common goal, just a switch in focus, had a mammoth task in order to prepare for the new challenge ahead. The configuration of the Battalion remained the same, but the patrol equipment changed – from desert DPM to the scarlet

tunic and drill boots. Within 20 working days of returning from Afghanistan the Battalion was on parade in front of Her Majesty to be presented our New Colours. Every man oozing with pride as our Colonel-in-Chief inspected them with families looking on.

'The approach to this phase of the Operation from the boys underlined just how great they are, the success on Operations certainly stimulated them into realizing that success comes when the team works as one, no better example than the Birthday Parade. With memories of the tour still fresh, every man on parade giving that extra bit as if dedicating the parade to those that didn't come home with us.

'Personally the Queen's Birthday Parade was a fantastic challenge and privilege, having the opportunity to draw my sword for the only time as a Non-Commissioned Officer.

'I cannot begin to describe the pride I have in the Battalion for the success on Operations and on Ceremonial Duties.'

The Commanding Officer demonstrating excellent equestrian skills.

L/Sgt Roderick Tracey and L/Sgt Arron Harris / No 2 Company, Wellington Barracks

'I think the reality of what was to come hit us early in the year (2010) when we were still operating in Nad-e Ali district. After we got the message about The Queen's Birthday Parade we knew the Master Tailor and his team were already making preparations in SHAWQUAT at Battlegroup Headquarters ready for our return to London.'

The Jallow Brothers / The Queen's Company, Wellington Barracks

'It's an honour to parade on The Queen's Birthday with my brother. He is the one who talked me into joining.
We served together in Afghanistan and now on the Troop. He's been a real big brother.'

Before the parade.

The three Parades running up to the Troop.
'You look good, be good!'
'You look great, you are great!'
'You look fantastic, be fantastic!'

Captain Rupert Stevens / The Queen's Company, Wellington Barracks

'It has been an extremely busy but rewarding year, and what better way to have our homecoming parade than on Horse Guards in the presence of the entire Royal Family at Her Majesty's Birthday?'

Captain Howard Cordle / Subaltern of No 3 Guard on the Troop, Wellington Barracks

'What a joy to be on parade again, and with another layer on top of my tunic for good measure! Obviously this time we're rehearsing for the Troop in capes, just in case it should rain on the big day in June … not such a good look, but all for Queen and country!'

'Remove Capes!'

'Brollies Up!'

In the rehearsals leading up to the Troop the Grenadiers perform to an empty Horse Guards.

Gdsm Keith Wells and Gdsm Michael Piantkinskyj / Regimental Combat Medical Technicians, Wellington Barracks

On tour or on the parade ground the medics are always on hand for their guys,
providing medical cover as quickly as possible while also trying to maintain the dignity of a colleague.

L/Cpl Kamal (Rico) Richards / The Queen's Company, Wellington Barracks

'The build-up phases to the Troop, ie the training, is very hard going, due to the fact that we have to keep rehearsing all the time, and most weekends are taken away because of our duties. I guess it goes with the saying, work hard and you will reap the benefits in the end.'

CSM Steve (Treacle) Williams / Company Sergeant Major of The Queen's Company, Wellington Barracks

'GET ON PARADE!'
Another rehearsal, just weeks after returning from Afghanistan!

Lieutenant Mike Dobbin and Lieutenant Garth Banks watch the Battalion form up.

The Commanding Officer.

The Garrison Sgt Major has a brief discussion with the Commanding Officer before the parade starts.

HM The Queen and HRH Prince Philip arrive on Horse Guards Parade.

The Inspection.

The March Past In Quick Time.

The Commanding Officer, HRH The Regimental Colonel and HM The Colonel in Chief.

Sgt Dale Benison / The Inkerman Company, Wellington Barracks

'A proud day for me as a Platoon Sergeant, as I've worked day in and day out with these soldiers in adverse and challenging conditions during a rewarding tour of Afghanistan. Now I stand proud along side these men, participating in a great and memorable day.'

9 GRENADIER GUARDS HERITAGE: THE GUARDS MUSEUM
WELLINGTON BARRACKS, LONDON

Nations and dynasties throughout the ages have conveyed their history, culture and ethos through the medium of storytelling. The Guards are no different and their story, covering three and a half centuries, is told at The Guards Museum. The museum's primary aim is to help educate young Guardsmen in their heritage and then to help the public understand the close and personal relationship that exists between the Sovereign and the five Foot Guard regiments that protect her and her palaces. Located between the Guards' operational headquarters, Wellington Barracks, and the Guards Chapel, the spiritual home of the Guards Division, the museum is well worth a visit to learn more about these extraordinary units.

The State Colour. One of only two held within the British Army, it was given to the Grenadier Guards by HM Queen Victoria.

A ledger from the reformation of the British Army in 1660, commissioned by King Charles II whilst in exile in France.

This page, signed by King Charles II, pertains to the formation of 'his Majesties Foote Regiment of Guards'.
They were later to be styled The Grenadier Guards after the defeat of the Grenadiers of the French Imperial Guard at the Battle of Waterloo.

De Company!
This brick is an exact replica of 'The Brick' taken from Hougoumont Farm at the Battle of Waterloo. To this day the Brick is paraded around the Grenadiers barracks on a yearly basis by the Sergeants' Mess. The junior ranks try to gain control of the brick and retrieve it to the Corporals' Mess. In an often ungainly struggle this Brick seems to have played its part.

The man with the Golden Gun.
A 24-carat gold pin that sits on the medals of the best rifle shot within the Regiment.

WITH SPECIAL THANKS TO...

Major Grant Baker and Lieutenant Colonel Roly Walker for making this book possible.

All members of the First Battalion who allowed me to photograph them throughout the year, and especially to those who are quoted in the book, for adding insight by giving their thoughts and experiences.

Captain John Donaldson, IG, for overseeing a smooth and whisky-free trip to Afghanistan.

Captain James Fox, Captain Rupert Stevens, Captain Alex Bayliss, Major Ed Paintin, Major Alex Cartwright, Major Rich Green, Padre Jason Clarke and Sergeant Major Ian Farrell.

The Guards Museum, in particular Andrew Wallis.

Buckingham Palace.

The Regimental Association.

The Media Ops Staff at the MOD, for their help and guidance.

Matt, Chris and everyone at Third Millennium for their hard work and professionalism.

Warren Du-Preez, Nick Thornton Jones and Giles Price for inspiring me to be a better photographer.

Finally to my Mother, Father, family and friends for their love and ongoing support.

© 2011 Grenadier Guards and Third Millennium Publishing Ltd
Photographs © 2011 Algenon Brinton

First published in 2011 by Third Millennium Publishing Limited, a subsidiary of Third Millennium Information Limited

2–5 Benjamin Street
London
United Kingdom
EC1M 5QL
www.tmiltd.com

ISBN 978 1 906507 73 2

British Library Cataloguing in Publication Data:
A CIP catalogue record for this book is available from the British Library.

Edited and photographed by Algy Brinton
Designed by Matthew Wilson
Production by Bonnie Murray
Reprographics by Studio Fasoli, Italy
Printed by Gorenjski Tisk, Slovenia